Elias Hicks

a Controversial Quaker

by

Simon Webb

© 2016 Simon Webb

The right of Simon Webb to be
identified as the Author of the Work
has been asserted by him in accordance
with the Copyright, Designs
and Patents Act 1988.

All rights reserved.

Revised and corrected edition published
by the Langley Press, 2016

The cover shows a photograph of a bust
of Elias Hicks by William Ordway Partridge,
and a letter in Hicks' handwriting

More Quaker books from the Langley Press:

The Captivity of Elizabeth Hanson, Written by Samuel Bownas: A Quaker Abducted by Native Americans in 1725

George Fox in Barbados: With the Complete Text of the Letter to the Governor of Barbados

Deep Roots? A Fresh Look at the Origins of some Quaker Ideas

Quakers, Newgate and the Old Bailey

Open House: A Quaker Tale in Verse

The Quaker Sonnets

The Theology of Small Things

For free downloads and more from the Langley Press, visit our website at:

http://tinyurl.com/lpdirect

CONTENTS

I: Leaving an Impression — 5

II: Getting Away From It All — 11

III. Finding a Voice — 19

IV: The Great Cause — 28

V: The Minister In Action — 38

VI: Misgivings — 54

VII: Conflict — 64

VIII: Dust Settling — 72

IX: Last Days — 84

Select Bibliography — 88

I: LEAVING AN IMPRESSION

In the spring of 1830, a macabre scene began to unfold itself in the Quaker burial ground at Jericho, Long Island. The details of the story have become vague over the years, but the heart of what happened is that a group of three men, led by one Samuel F. Clements, dug up the freshly-buried body of the man who had until recently been Jericho's most famous living resident.

The diggers, who probably worked by night, were not intending to steal the body or anything buried with it – their plan was to make a death-mask of the deceased.

A little historical imagination is needed to fill out the picture. As we squint into the dense fog of time, we can discern a man with a shovel working away at the new grave by the light of lamps set on the ground, or hung over the side of the excavation as the work progresses. Another man, directed to keep a look-out, scans the surrounding darkness for approaching lights.

As the coffin is carefully raised to the surface, one of the men, an Italian plasterer, is busy mixing the plaster-of-paris that will be applied to the face of the dead man. As the body is laid at the edge of the grave, the plaster-of-paris man works the white mixture into every nook and cranny of the face, then covers his work with gauze and a final coat of plaster. Once the plaster has been put on, there is an agonising wait while Clements himself, perhaps, reads his pocket-watch by the light of a lantern, making sure enough time has elapsed for the plaster to be truly dry.

After the deed was done and the old man put back in his grave, word of the unauthorised mask-taking came to the ears of local friends of the deceased, who dug him up again and found that, yes, there were traces of plaster in his hair.

Samuel Clements, the leader of the diggers, was a local postmaster and editor of a Brooklyn-based newspaper called the *Long Island Patriot*. Clements employed the young Walt Whitman, a native of Long Island and later a great poet, as a 'printer's devil'. Whitman described Clements as a 'lank, lean, eccentric hook-nosed Quaker and Southerner'. That Clements had drifted away from the true Quaker path is evident from his activities that night. Contemporaries would also have recognised his lapsed condition in his jazzy blue waistcoat with the brass buttons, and his habit of attending the 'great old rough, fortress-looking stone'[1] Dutch Reformed Church in Joralemon Street, Brooklyn.

Something called the death-mask of Elias Hicks is held at the library of Swarthmore College in Pennsylvania. The face is long and strongly

---

[1] Description by Whitman printed in his *Autobiographia: selected from his prose writings,* Putnam, 1892

aquiline, with heavy eyebrows. Although there is some doubt about the provenance of the mask, is does resemble portraits made of Elias Hicks during his life, including one by Henry Inman which was said by Walt Whitman to be a 'wonderful likeness'.

Of course, the portraits of Hicks add details that would not be seen in a death-mask – long hair above a high forehead, parted in the middle and swept behind large, intelligent ears. The clothing Hicks wears in his portraits is striking – it seems to belong to an earlier age than that in which he lived and died. As a Plain Quaker (a breed of Quaker that is rare in the twenty-first century) Elias Hicks wore unfashionable, unadorned clothes in unassuming colours, including 'drab', the slightly brownish light grey that has now given its name to anything dull.

According to Whitman, Clements and his co-conspirators planned to make some money by selling portrait busts of the famous Quaker, based on the death-mask. Unfortunately the men fell out over the distribution of the cash, and all the busts were destroyed. The death-mask itself may have influenced the later bust created by the sculptor William Ordway Partridge. This is a beautifully-made and inspiring portrait of Hicks which, from certain angles, seems to suggest the wisdom and smiling patience of some statues of the Buddha.

Partridge's bust is so life-like that the photograph of it reproduced in Henry Wilbur's 1910 biography of Hicks looks disconcertingly like a photograph of the man himself – a man who died nearly ten years before any practical system of photography had been introduced.

Elias Hicks died at the age of eighty-one: if he had lived to be ninety, someone might have asked him to sit for a photograph, as the Daguerreotype system of photography was in use by the late 1830s. The chances are, though, that Hicks would not have sat still so that his features could be painted by light onto a silver plate. As a Plain Quaker, allergic to anything vain, he seems never to have sat for his portrait and, as a result, all images of him made during his life were derived from sketches made without his knowledge.

The American painter Henry Ketcham made a full-length portrait painting of Hicks, based on studies made while the artist sat in the galleries of Quaker Meeting-Houses where Hicks was present. Unfortunately, fire damaged the bottom part of this picture. The scorched portion was cut away, and we now have only the head and shoulders. The remaining fragment is an acceptable portrait of Hicks, but it does show that Ketcham was a very unsophisticated artist. Both Inman and Ketcham present us with rather grim images of Elias.

While artists and plasterers tried to steal Hicks' likeness, stenographers such as the extravagantly named Marcus Tullius Cicero Gould tried to record his spoken words using the phonetic squiggles of short-hand. Like Ketcham, Gould also sat in the galleries of Meeting-Houses. One result of Gould's labours was a book published in 1825 called *A series of Extemporaneous Discourses Delivered in the Several Meetings of the Society of Friends in Philadelphia, Germantown, Abington, Byberry, Newtown, Falls and Trenton by Elias Hicks*. In their introductory advertisement to this volume, the publishers state that parts of some of the discourses may not have been recorded accurately, 'in consequence of an unfavourable position for hearing, occupied by the stenographer, in very crowded assemblies, together with his want of acquaintance with the voice and manner of the speaker, and his rapid utterance'. Like the artists, Gould the stenographer recorded Hicks without his permission.

The portraits and stenographic recordings of Hicks are somewhat unreliable, as are written accounts of him by his contemporaries, whether they counted themselves among his friends or his enemies. We do, however, have a body of writings by Hicks himself, in the form of his *Journal* (recently republished by by the Inner Light Press), his letters, and other pieces published during his lifetime.

The fact that people like Gould and Ketcham, and the resurrection men of that night in the burial ground, took such pains to record something of Hicks shows how important his contemporaries believed him to be. In his biography of Hicks published in 1910, Henry Watson Wilbur states that 'few men in their day were more talked about than Elias Hicks', and that 'interest in his person and in his preaching continued for years after his death'. In his account of time spent with Walt Whitman while the poet was preparing, among other things, his *Notes* on Hicks, Horace Traubel[2] refers to the Long Island Quaker simply as 'Hicks' when he first mentions him, as if he expected his readers to be able to identify the subject of Whitman's essay from his surname alone. And Traubel's book was published nearly eighty years after Hicks' death.

Hicks is still remembered today, although knowledge of him is almost entirely limited to Members of the Religious Society of Friends, and other people with an interest in the history and ideas of the Quakers. Among Quakers, Hicks is remembered as one of the figures central to the painful split in that Society that occurred in America in the 1820s. One purpose of this book is to show that there was more to the Jericho Quaker than the qualities and utterances that put him near the eye of that particular storm.

---

[2] *With Walt Whitman in Camden,* 1906

II: GETTING AWAY FROM IT ALL

Hicks is a very old English surname, which may go all the way back to the twelfth century. In the fourteenth century, Elias' ancestor Ellis Hicks was knighted on the battlefield of Poitiers in France. A Robert Hicks arrived in Massachusetts in 1621, and John Hicks came to live in the town of Hempstead on Long Island in 1640. It seems that none of Elias Hicks' forebears were Quakers until his father John became convinced. Thomas, the great-grandfather of Elias, was the first judge of Queen's County, Long Island: he offered great comfort and encouragement to the English Quaker minister Samuel Bownas when he was imprisoned on trumped-up charges at Jamaica, Long Island in 1702.

There have been Quakers on Long Island since 1657, when the island was part of the Dutch colony of New Netherlands. New York, just a short ferry-ride away, was called New Amsterdam in those days. When Elias was born the Island, which is now one of the most heavily-populated places in the United States, was a predominantly rural part of the British Empire.

Elias Hicks was born at Hempstead, Long Island on the nineteenth of May, 1748. Elias was the fourth child of John and Martha Hicks, who had six children altogether – all of them boys. One of Hicks' cousins was the noted painter Edward Hicks, who was, like Elias, a Quaker Minister. Although there were plenty of Quakers on the Island at this time, the Hickses didn't live near any, and Elias was forced to mix with other children who belonged to 'the world's people'. In his *Journal*, he tells us that this led him into many temptations, but his tender conscience kept him more or less on the straight and narrow.

As a small child, Hicks had a vision of hell in a recurring dream, the horror of which seemed to reinforce the protective power of his conscience. In the dream, he approached a wren's nest in the hollow of an old tree, hoping to steal the eggs. As he reached into the hollow, he saw the face of an angel, and then fire blazed up out of the tree and surrounded him.

The family moved further south on the Island when Elias was about eight years old, to settle on a seaside farm at Rockaway: the farm had been given to Elias' father by his own father, Jacob. Here there were also opportunities for wild behaviour, especially when Elias' mother died and the children were left in the care of his father's rather playful niece.

Elias was, however, kept out of trouble by the lure of the marshes near the family's new home. There he could fish, and shoot the local water-fowl. Today, when so many Friends are vegetarians, or otherwise concerned about animal welfare, this kind of thing would hardly be regarded as a very suitable occupation for a Quaker child. Elias was, however, a farm boy, accustomed to the use of animals as sources of food, clothing and other necessities. Hunting and fishing also kept the young Elias out of trouble, and they taught him patience, an ability to be alone, and an appreciation for nature.

Walt Whitman makes the local wildlife part of the evocative picture of old Long Island he includes in his *Notes* on Elias Hicks.

How well I remember the region - the flat plains of the middle of Long Island, as then, with their prairie-like vistas and grassy patches in every direction, and the 'kill-calf'[3] and herds of cattle and sheep. Then the South Bay and shores and the salt meadows, and the sedgy smell, and numberless little bayous and hummock-islands in the waters, the habitat of every sort of fish and aquatic fowl of North America.

One summer, when Hicks was only thirteen, he went to stay with one of his married elder brothers, and found himself quite outside the control of any responsible adult. He was tall enough to be able to pass as an older boy, and began to hang out with young men, to play cards and to ride in horse-races.

Elias's early exposure to the ways of the world's people, when he knew he was a Quaker himself, may have contributed to his later determination to

---

[3] A poisonous shrub found on the Island.

keep Quakers and non-Quakers apart. This Quaker insularity was a feature of Friends' life in those days that we would now be more likely to associate with groups such as the Amish, or the Hutterites.

Hicks particularly disliked the idea of schools where Quaker and non-Quaker children could mix. This seems narrow-minded today, but Quakers like Hicks were convinced that their own way of life contained some unique and valuable elements that needed to be preserved from any process of dilution. The worst symptom of this enthusiastic cultivation of the hedge around the Quakers, by the Quakers themselves, was the widespread practice of disowning Friends who had 'married out'.

The Quakers weren't just trying to stop non-Quakers entering their world - Quakers setting out to be chummy with the world's people could come up against prejudice, and its usual accompaniment, ignorance. For Friends, meeting non-Friends socially must have been very awkward at times. The Quakers dressed differently from other Americans, and to some extent spoke in their own jargon, parts of which must have been impenetrable to outsiders. They were wary of alcohol, and some didn't smoke, or touch stimulants such as tea. At a formal dinner, they might not have cried 'amen' at the end of grace, preferring their own silent grace. If there was dancing after dinner, the Quakers would for the most part have stood around like grey wallflowers.

The Quaker men would usually wear their

characteristic broad-brimmed hats indoors, and would not even take them off as a mark of respect if they met somebody – no bowing and scraping for them.

Hicks didn't like to see farm-boys from Long Island running off to make their fortunes in New York, whether in commerce or public service, and in later life he firmly objected to the laying of the railway-lines that would tie the Island closer to its cosmopolitan neighbour. He seemed to feel that the Quaker communities on Long Island had at least a chance of living perfect Quaker lives in their scattered farms and settlements. To judge from his own writings, it would seem that Hicks' family sometimes got close to this ideal of quiet contentment.

At seventeen, Hicks was apprenticed to a carpenter – a very suitable trade for a Christian if ever there was one. Masters were expected to look to the moral nurture of their young apprentices, but although Hicks' master was a good Quaker man, he was so busy that he was, as Hicks says in his *Journal* 'of little use to me in my religious improvement'. Later, Hicks was to add the trade of surveyor to his personal store of skills.

Up to this point, the life of Elias Hicks resembles, in many ways, that of the founder of Quakerism, George Fox. Both came from respected, reasonably well-off country families, and both were apprenticed – in Fox's case to a shoemaker who also kept sheep. Both were aware of temptation in early life, and both were kept in line by an active conscience. Both seem to have had a sense that they were set apart in some way, and both were puzzled at times about the nature of, or reason for, their 'apartness'.

Hicks didn't spend his carpenter's apprenticeship at a bench in a workshop – his master dragged him and his other workers all over the place, wherever he was called to work. Since many of the Long Island houses at this time were made of wood, it is not surprising that the carpenters were kept busy.

On his travels, Hicks could not help but notice a curious custom, called 'bundling', that was practiced among the local people. In English playground slang, a 'bundle' is a fight, but the American version seems to have been quite the opposite. On Sunday evenings, it seems, the young people were allowed to spend hours in 'vain amusements', after which they would 'couple out' and spend the night sleeping together. Hicks implies that these young people were not married, and he found the practice another temptation, as well he might. Even Quaker parents allowed 'bundling', Hicks tells us.

This highly risky custom may have been an American survival of a tradition from old Europe, which may itself have gone back to pagan times. In some cultures, sex before marriage was considered quite normal, even when the area in question had been ostensibly Christian for hundreds of years. On the English island of Portland, for instance, a couple could not marry unless the girl was already pregnant.

As well as continuing with his horse-racing and card-playing, Hicks developed a taste for dancing, but his sense of the wickedness of this 'unnatural and unchristian practice' eventually persuaded him to give it up. In his wild days (according to Walt Whitman) Hicks was often to be found in the company of Whitman's great-grandfather at 'merry-makings and sleigh-rides in winter over "the plains"'.

At twenty-one, Hicks had finished his apprenticeship, and was well on the way to becoming a rather serious young man. He attended Quaker Meetings more regularly, and avoided temptation by his old method of fishing; and 'fowling', in other words, shooting birds. When he was alone on these expeditions, he now found himself 'taken up in divine meditations' during those periods when it was necessary for him to wait in silence. When he hunted in company, he grew to dislike the practice of shooting birds just for sport, and resolved only to kill animals that would be useful when dead. This is similar to the conscientious concern for animals expressed by the saintly eighteenth-century New Jersey Quaker, John Woolman. In other respects, Elias Hicks also followed in the footsteps of Woolman, although it is hard to imagine two Quakers of more different characters: Hicks outspoken, bold and decisive; Woolman cautious, courteous and tender.

In 1771, at the age of twenty-two, Elias married.

His bride was Jemima Seaman, a Quaker girl just two years younger than her groom, daughter of substantial farmers at Jericho, Long Island. Jemima was an only child, which meant that there were no Seaman brothers to help out round the farm or in the tannery business Hicks' father-in-law also owned. The Seamans had, however, now acquired a son by marriage, and it was natural that, a few months after their marriage, the young couple should have been invited to live in Jemima's childhood home.

The Seaman family had been Quakers since the 1680s, and were probably among the first Quakers on Long Island. By marrying Jemima and going to live at Jericho, Elias Hicks was immersing himself in a place where Quaker culture was all-pervasive.

III. FINDING A VOICE

Elias Hicks now threw himself into work at his father-in-law's farm, and into work and worship at the local Quaker Meeting House, which he tells us was only three miles away.

Then as now, there were two main types of meeting in Quakerism. There were Meetings for Business and Meetings for Worship, the latter sometimes called 'Public Meetings'. Meetings for Worship are the Quaker equivalents of church services, while Business Meetings are the equivalents of church councils, steering groups, standing committees, synods, annual general meetings, etc. among non-Quaker Christians.

Hicks began to take an active part in Business Meetings, both at the level of his local Quaker Meeting in Jericho and in the wider area. The business of the 'wider area' would have been discussed at Monthly Meetings, while the concerns of the Meeting at Jericho would have been covered by Preparative Meetings. Hicks spoke at Preparative and Monthly Meetings, but crossed a sort of personal Rubicon when he began to speak at Public Meetings for Worship.

The format of Quaker Meetings for Worship in

Hicks' day would have been much the same as Meetings in Britain today, except that Meetings would often go on for much longer than the single hour that is customary now. The Friends sat in silence, sometimes for a whole Meeting, but anyone could stand and speak, or 'give Ministry', if he *or she* felt inspired to do so.

The 'or she' part was a distinctive feature of Quakerism in those days, when groups such as the Anglicans still had a long way to go before they allowed women to become ministers. In Hicks' time, however, the women still sat separately from the men during Meetings for Worship, and Business Meetings were usually divided along gender lines.

To allow Meeting Houses to be used for business and for worship, sliding partitions or shutters were often installed so that the men's and women's Business Meetings could be held separately. During worship, the Elders and Ministers of the meeting also sat separately, in the Elders gallery – usually just a few rows of benches raised up like seats in a theatre, complete with hand-rails.

Some Quakers attend Meetings for Worship for years and never speak, whereas some speak very regularly. In Hicks' day, Ministry was supposed to be inspired by the Holy Spirit, and in Samuel Bownas's guide for Quaker Ministers[4] he tackles the important question of how the speaker is supposed to know if the Spirit has indeed inspired him or her,

---

[4] Bownas, S. *A Description of the Qualification Necessary to a Gospel Minister* Pendle Hill Publications, 1989

or if the Minister's motivation is something less worthy.

Personal doubt as to whether one's Ministry is inspired from the right place is something that stops many Quakers from speaking – another factor is the expectation that, in a regular Meeting for Worship, the Ministry should be quite unprepared, with little or none of it read from a written text.

At first, Hicks was fearful of giving Ministry in Public Meetings, but at last he made an attempt, and was rewarded with a feeling of 'joy and sweet consolation' when he had said his piece.

Above the level of the Preparative and Monthly Meetings, there were and are also Quarterly Meetings, and at the top of the pyramid, Yearly Meetings – 'AGMs' populated by representatives from a group of Monthly Meetings, and by visitors from other Yearly Meetings. In Britain, Quakerism in the whole country was and is dominated by one Yearly Meeting – now called Britain Yearly Meeting, but known as London Yearly Meeting in Hicks' time. Hicks' local Preparative and Monthly Meetings came under the jurisdiction of New York Yearly Meeting.

The main thing that has to be remembered about this hierarchy of Meetings is that a Monthly, Quarterly or Yearly Meeting in the Quaker world is not just the Business Meeting that happens, say, once a year, in the case of a Yearly Meeting. In Quaker terms, a Yearly Meeting also refers to the *Quaker area* that this Meeting has jurisdiction over.

These geographical Yearly Meetings are the Quaker equivalents of dioceses in the Anglican or Roman Catholic churches. Quarterly, Monthly and Preparative Meetings are geographical sub-sections of a Yearly Meeting's area, the Preparative Meeting usually covering just one Meeting-House and its members.

One result of all these Meetings for Worship and for Business was that active Quakers were often obliged to travel around from Meeting to Meeting; a strenuous activity which Hicks was soon involved in. This type of travel became more hazardous when the American Revolutionary War[5] broke out in 1775, when Elias Hicks was twenty-seven years old, and had been married for four years. By this time, Elias and Jemima had three children; Martha, David, and another Elias.

During the war, Long Island was held by troops on the British side, whereas the mainland was held by the American army. The Quakers of those days were, however, easily recognisable as Quakers because of their distinctive clothing and speech, and, because they were known to be a peaceful people, they were allowed to pass through the lines of the armies without hindrance. Hicks himself passed through in this way six times, and was not even molested by what he calls the 'cruel unprincipled banditti' who dwelt in no-man's land.

In 1779 Hicks travelled through no-man's-land on his way to Philadelphia Yearly Meeting. He and

---

[5] Called the American War of Independence in Britain.

his companions saw desolate and empty settlements, ghost-towns where grass grew in the streets. Hicks and his companions were going to Philadelphia Yearly Meeting at this time because their own Yearly Meeting of New York had referred a tricky case to the senior meeting. This involved the cellar of the new Meeting-House in New York, which had been rented out to the British army as storage space during the Revolutionary War. Eventually it was decided that it had been a mistake to let part of a building belonging to a peace church be used for 'warlike stores' and the rent money was returned.

The year before, Hicks had been recorded as a Minister among the Quakers, which meant that he was now the equivalent of a preacher or clergyman among non-Quaker Christians. This appointment was not attached to any kind of salary or stipend, however, and it certainly didn't come with anything like a vicarage, a special set of clothes or a title such as 'Reverend' prefixed to Hicks' name. Hicks had merely been recognised as a giver of valuable Ministry, and his new status meant that he was expected to continue to use his gift. This was an expectation that Hicks did not disappoint.

In 1777 Jemima's parents had died, which meant that she and Elias were now in charge of the Seaman farm. In the same year, Jemima gave birth to her fourth child, Elizabeth, who died very young, in 1779, of smallpox. A third daughter, Phebe, was born in the same year, but despite his responsibilities at home, it was in 1779 that Hicks began, in Quaker parlance, to 'travel in the Ministry'.

The first Quaker, George Fox, travelled in the Ministry or, as non-Quakers might say, worked as an itinerant preacher. Fox travelled all over the British Isles, and even ventured onto the European mainland. He covered vast distances in the Americas and, as we shall see, he also spent time on the Caribbean island of Barbados.

Hicks, like many other Quaker Ministers before and since, took his message on the road, but, in his case, he never strayed out of the North American Continent. This vast area did, however, allow him to clock up enormous mileages – he could be gone for months at a time, and regularly travelled over a thousand miles per trip. This was all accomplished on horseback or in carriages of some kind, over poor roads, some of them nothing more than old Indian trails that were barely distinguishable from the surrounding terrain.

Hicks stayed for the most part within the areas that would become the United States, but the States themselves expanded during the time of his Ministry. In 1800, when Hicks was fifty-two, there were only sixteen states. This number had grown to twenty-four by the time of Hicks' death.

Hicks lived during the period known to Quaker historians as the Great Migration. This saw thousands of Friends from the southern and eastern states making their way into territories such as those that became the states of Ohio and Indiana. The Quakers of the south migrated partly because they could no longer live in a society where slavery was still prevalent. According to Rufus Jones[6], many Friends from the north-east were motivated to move by idealism, as well as the classic yearnings for adventure and a better life.

Many of these Quaker migrants journeyed in the convoys of covered wagons familiar from hundreds of western films. When they finally settled, they had to cope with tough conditions and, in many cases, profound isolation. The more enterprising Quaker Ministers, such as Elias Hicks and Stephen Grellet, were soon visiting these pioneer settlements and putting them back into contact with the Quaker world.

Perhaps because little work could be done about the farm in winter, Hicks was quite prepared to travel during the coldest part of the year, crossing frozen lakes and rivers, on wooden sledges that sometimes broke, or had to be dug out of snow-drifts. At times the weather was so bad that it was not even possible to cross between Long Island and the mainland, a crossing that had not yet been spanned by the celebrated Brooklyn Bridge.

Much of Hicks' *Journal* is taken up with his travels, during which he generally paid his own travel expenses, but usually ate and slept at the houses of local fellow-Quakers, which, even if he had offered something in return for his bed and

---

[6] *The Later Periods of Quakerism*, Volume I, Macmillan, 1921

board, would still have reduced his costs considerably. That Hicks felt able to leave his farm for long periods suggests that the old Seaman place was large enough and profitable enough for there to be sufficient skilled hands to do the work, and not miss Elias' contribution. It also shows that Jemima was a very capable woman, worthy to be trusted with such a responsibility. Although Elias might be hundreds of miles away from home, the farm was often in his thoughts, however, and he would pepper his letters home with hints and reminders of what needed doing.

At home in Jericho, Hicks was frequently busy with Quaker work, which also suggests that the house and farm were well-staffed. When the local Quaker school failed to attract a teacher, Elias even found time to act as a temporary schoolmaster.

One might have expected that Jemima and Elias' four sons could have helped out around the farm, but, tragically, this was not to be the case. David, Elias, Jonathan and John all suffered from a condition which Paul Buckley, the most recent editor of Hicks' *Journal*, suggests was 'a sex-linked recessive type of muscular dystrophy'. This meant that none of them could walk after their ninth or tenth year, and all of them died in their teens. Buckley notes that Elias Willets, Hicks' first grandson, suffered from the same disease. He also speculates that this condition may have been connected in some way to the fact that Jemima was an only child. Strange to say, Walt Whitman, Hicks' great admirer and fellow Long-Islander, also suffered from a hereditary form of paralysis that killed his brother, and caused him much frustration in later life.

The wealth and generosity of the Hickses is demonstrated by the fact that they were able to run the farm on a very ethical basis. Elias refused to profiteer when prices were high, continuing to sell his wheat at a dollar a bushel one year, when speculators offered him three dollars. He also distributed food and firewood to his neighbours, in times of need.

In his 1956 biography of Hicks, Bliss Forbush speculates that the farm in Jericho would have been self-sufficient in many things, which would have cut domestic expenditure. As a plain people, the Quakers of those days would have had little to spend money on, since they were wary of alcohol, and avoided tobacco, fancy food, elaborate clothes and entertainments such as the theatre, dances, gambling and musical concerts. We shall see that the Hickses also avoided the dangerous luxuries called sugar and tobacco. As a result of all these factors, Hicks never seems to have been strapped for cash.

IV THE GREAT CAUSE

Until the year 1811, Elias Hicks had lived an admirable life, having grown out of his youthful temptations and taken up the responsibilities of a farm, a family and his Quaker work, including his work as an itinerant Minister. He had not, however, done anything that was likely to make him so famous that, after his death, people would dig up his body to make a plaster-cast of his face. In 1811, though, all this was to change.

In that year, Elias Hicks was sixty-three; an age at which many people in the twenty-first century would start to think about retirement: it was, however, a characteristic of Hicks' life that the most important things he did, and the most important things that happened to him, came to him when he already had many years on his back.

What happened in 1811 was that, after over thirty years of vocal Ministry, Hicks put some of his words into a short book with a long title: *Observations on the Slavery of the Africans and Their Descendants, and on the Use of the Produce of their Labour*. The publication was prompted by events at the New York Yearly Meeting of 1810. There, the Quakers chose to erase all mention of 'prize goods' from their Book of Discipline. This meant that the New York Quakers were, in effect, relieving themselves of the responsibility of not buying, or trading in, goods captured in war or made by slaves.

Although the Quakers have never had a set creed that all members had to agree with, different Yearly Meetings have always produced Books of Discipline, which lay down how Quaker Meetings of different types should be run, and offer advice to Friends on how they should live their lives. As the world changes, these books of discipline are subject to revision, but the change the New York Quakers made in 1810 did not meet with the approval of Elias Hicks.

The Quaker advice against buying or selling prize goods was long-established: the prohibition on purchasing or dealing in such goods was part of the Quaker stance against war itself, but in early nineteenth-century America, prize goods were also understood to include the produce of slaves, and the slaves themselves, who were still bought and sold in some parts of the United States at that time.

As Hicks asserts in his *Observations*, many Africans who were later sold into slavery had first lost their freedom in Africa when they had become prisoners of war. Hicks considered that the acts of cruelty and violence that were used to control the slaves were themselves acts of war – the produce of the slaves therefore counted as prize goods, and it was his opinion that the Quakers should not touch such produce.

The New York Quakers had removed the advice about prize goods from their Discipline because, they claimed, it was difficult to distinguish between goods produced by slaves and those made by free workers. Hicks' answer to this problem was to advise everyone to avoid rice, sugar and cotton, all of which came from plants that, in North America, could only be grown in the southern states, where slavery was practised on a very large scale.

From the text of a speech delivered by one Barnabas Bates[7] in New York, just a couple of weeks after the death of Hicks, it emerges that the man from Jericho also spoke against the use of tobacco, not just because it was cultivated by slaves, but also because he believed that tobacco itself was poisonous. Hicks was also concerned by the way that tobacco made the smoker thirsty, and tempted him to drink alcoholic drinks. It is interesting to note that Bates' speech, which was later reprinted in *The Friend* and as a short pamphlet, was delivered to an audience of both white and black people in New York. Hicks' efforts did not go unnoticed by the people he was trying to help.

Hicks implied that those who bought slave goods were participating in the crime of slavery, and were, in effect, employing the slave-owners as their agents.

Hicks' *Observations* takes the form of a series of

---

[7] Printed as *Remarks on the character and exertions of Elias Hicks in the abolition of slavery...* New York, 1830

questions to which the author provides answers. When his imaginary questioner protests that the guilt of an individual consumer of slave goods is tiny because of the scale of the consumption of these goods, Hicks replies with the assertion that, however much the guilt is divided up, each consumer's personal quantity of guilt remains the same. Hicks gives the example of a murder victim who is stabbed by a hundred people at the same time – all one hundred assassins are equally guilty.

As well as warning people away from slave goods, Hicks uses his *Observations* to remind his readers that slavery should not be encouraged, because his readers themselves would not like to be enslaved. To back up this idea, Hicks quotes Matthew 7:12: 'All things whatsoever ye would that men should do to you, do ye even so to them'. He also cites Ezekiel 18:4 to prove that all men are born free, because their souls belong to God: 'All souls are mine; as the soul of the father, so also the soul of the son is mine...'

Hicks expands on the idea that people should only treat other people as they themselves would like to be treated by imagining what it would be like if slave-traders regularly kidnapped white people from the northern United States and sold them into slavery. This approach allows him to describe, in powerfully emotive sentences, the horrors of the slave-trade:

We behold the fond children, with ghastly look and

frighted eyes, cling to their beloved parents, not to be separated from them, but by the lash of their cruel drivers...

Hicks uses the idea that, under God, Africans are equal to people of white European descent, to argue that, even where local laws allow slavery, slavery should be considered a crime and the slave-owners criminals. He also criticises the New York law that stated that children born to slaves in that city would be legally free. For Hicks, this law does not go far enough: he wants all the slaves in New York to be set free, and, furthermore, he wants the freed slaves to be compensated financially for the unpaid labour they have done as slaves. He also suggests that their ex-masters should provide for the education of the children of freed slaves.

None of the ideas Hicks put across in his *Observations* were new to Quakerdom: what set the *Observations* apart were the reputation of the author, the righteous anger evident in the writing, and the historic moment at which the pamphlet was published.

The *Observations* came at a time when the temperature of Quaker anti-slavery activity was rather cooler than it had been in the middle of the eighteenth century. It was then that the saintly New Jersey Quaker John Woolman helped to rid American Quakers of the sin of slave-holding, a practice many Friends had clung to since the mid-seventeenth century, when Quakerism first began.

When George Fox visited Barbados in 1671, he failed to condemn slavery outright, although at that time and in that place slavery was present in its most pervasive and horrific form. In the *Epistle to the Governor of Barbados*, which Fox wrote with the assistance of some other Friends, he merely suggested that the white settlers should treat their slaves well, instruct them in Christianity and release them after a number of years.

For several generations after George Fox, Quakers continued to keep slaves, and it is clear that many did not even bother to follow the compassionate suggestions in Fox's *Epistle*. Although many Quaker individuals and groups spoke out against slavery, many defended it, or at least did not go out of their way to combat the practice.

When Hicks published his *Observations*, most American Quakers had been free of direct involvement with the slave trade for decades: Hicks' pamphlet was a reminder that they could go even further in encouraging the collapse of slavery.

The non-slave-owning Quakers may also have been resting on their laurels as far as slavery was concerned, because the importation of fresh African slaves had been prohibited in 1808, three years before the publication of the *Observations*. But it was very clear by 1811 that the natural increase in the slave population could supply demand for slaves in the southern states, where they were still legally owned.

The demand for slaves had increased after Eli Whitney patented his cotton gin (or 'cotton engine') in 1793. The gin meant that the cotton plants could be processed into cotton more quickly and efficiently, and that the short-staple variety of cotton could be grown more profitably. Since short-staple cotton could be grown in more northerly areas where the long-staple type could not have thrived, cotton cultivation in the United States grew exponentially, and the numbers of slaves needed grew with it.

The effect of the several editions of Hicks' *Observations* was considerable, and the pamphlet circulated widely, both inside and outside Quakerdom, in America and Europe. The Quakers' exclusive use of the produce of free labour was strengthened, and Hicks continued to speak against slavery in his Ministry.

Hicks' devotion to the cause of the African Americans went further than just preaching and publishing a book. Seventeen years before Hicks published his *Observations*, he had participated in the setting up of a charity designed to relieve the poverty of local Africans, and to provide for the education of their children. According to Wilbur, Hicks felt a responsibility to provide for the welfare of the Africans his father had owned as slaves, and made restitution to them for the crime of their enslavement. He also employed a black man called David in a responsible position on his farm for many years. David's mother Ellenor helped out around the house, and both she and David were remembered in Hicks' will. Hicks left them the equivalent of over twenty-six thousand dollars each in modern money.

In the depths of winter, Hicks would also deliver free vegetables and firewood to poor African neighbours on Long Island. He regularly preached to congregations of African and Native Americans, and of such a meeting at Easton, Maryland in 1798 he wrote that 'many of them [the Africans] appeared much higher in the kingdom than a great many of the whites'.

Like many anti-slavery campaigners of his generation, Hicks believed that there might be a case for 'repatriating' Africans to their 'native' continent, or encouraging them to set up black-only colonies, for instance in the American South-West. Today, such ideas smack of racism or even apartheid, but it must be remembered that many in the African Diaspora at the time longed for a 'return' to Africa itself. In the year of the publication of Hicks' *Observations*, the black American Quaker ship-owner Paul Cuffee set out on an expedition to 'return' a number of willing African Americans to Sierra Leone.

Elias Hicks lived to see a revival of action against slave goods that must have been inspired either directly or indirectly by his *Observations*. A free produce store was set up in Baltimore in 1826, and the state of Delaware saw the founding of its Free Labour Society. Philadelphia got its own antislavery magazine, the *African Observer*, and its own free produce society. The anti-slavery sentiment that Hicks had revived also encouraged Quakers in their efforts to free slaves, not least by smuggling them into the free states via the famous underground railroad.

The name of Hicks was so closely associated with the cause of African Americans that, in January 1830, the members of a newly-formed black burial society in New York decided to call themselves 'The New York African Hicks Association'.

From the long perspective of the twenty-first century, it seems inconceivable that any of Hicks' Quaker contemporaries could have objected to his teachings on slavery, but some did indeed take issue with them. There is no doubting the anger that Hicks expressed in his *Observations*, and it seems that in his public preaching on this and other subjects, the Long Island Quaker could be very outspoken. This aggressive tone, that caused Hicks to compare the buyers of slave-goods to murderers, seems to have ruffled the feathers of some of the Quaker-birds.

Somebody must have pointed out to the author of the *Observations* that, whereas Quakers in the free northern states could avoid the purchase of slave-goods, in the south so much of what was offered for sale was from the hands of slaves, that it was quite impossible for southern Friends to follow Hicks' teachings. Hicks therefore attached an extra paragraph to later editions of the *Observations*, absolving white southerners from guilt in this respect.

Hicks was not, however, prepared to soften his stance on slavery as it related to northern Quakers. In his Ministry to the Monthly Meeting at Pine Street, Philadephia, in 1819, Hicks was critical of the older Members of this Meeting in general, and very pointed in his remarks about how some of them had given up the idea of avoiding slave-goods. This Ministry from the Long Islander was resented by an Elder of that meeting called Jonathan Evans, who had indeed started to use the products of slavery again.

When Hicks went into the women's Meeting at Pine Street, Evans arranged for most of the Quakers in the men's Meeting to adjourn, so that when Hicks had finished speaking to the women, he returned to a nearly empty room. Hicks remarked to the few men who had stayed behind that 'it was kind of them to leave my coat behind when they went'.

Hicks might have been prepared for something like this snub in Philadelphia, since he had just come from Ohio Yearly Meeting, where Elisha Bates, of whom more later, had also criticised Hicks' stand against the use of slave goods. According to Henry Wilbur, Jonathan Evans had given up his own stance against slave goods when he decided that his feelings on this issue had emanated from his own will, and not from God. Visiting Hicks after the snub at Pine Street, Evans objected to Hicks calling Friends 'thieves and murderers' if they chose not to avoid slave goods.

V: THE MINISTER IN ACTION

Hicks' stand against slavery was entirely consistent with his theological views and, as we shall see, in both his Ministry and his writing he often used slavery as a specific illustration of what he had already described in more general terms. It is now time to take a closer look at two of the records of Hicks' sermons, to discover more about what the famous Minister actually said and did in Quaker Meetings.

The first of these pieces of Ministry was recorded by our friend the stenographer M.T.C. Gould on the eighth of December, 1824 at Byberry in Pennsylvania[8].

The first thing that strikes the modern Quaker about the initial section of Hicks' Ministry is its extreme length. It runs to nearly a thousand words, and, even allowing for Hicks' 'rapid utterance' it cannot have taken much less than an hour to deliver. By comparing this to other transcripts of Hicks' Ministry, it would appear that he regularly gave 'extemporaneous discourses' of this length, or longer. In the twenty-first century, a piece of

---
[8] Published in *A series of extemporaneous discourses, delivered in the several meetings of the Society of Friends...by Elias Hicks*, J. & E. Parker, 1825

Quaker Ministry will usually take up a few minutes at most – a speech of ten minutes would seem like a proper lecture. If Hicks had not been a good speaker, the assembled worshippers would surely have suffered on their hard wooden benches, especially if the Meeting-House was draughty, and let in some icy reminders of December in Pennsylvania.

Hicks would sometimes sit down after a piece of Ministry, then stand up and resume after a few minutes. This is actively discouraged in Britain Yearly Meeting today, and can look like 'hogging the floor' when it happens. It seems that Hicks' Byberry Ministry in 1824, which breaks up easily into three sections, was in fact punctuated by two silent 'rests', like the pauses between movements in a piece of classical music.

As well as the overall length of the Byberry Ministry, the length of some of Hicks' sentences is also surprising. Sentences of sixty words or more are not uncommon, and although this was not in evidence at Byberry, it would seem that Hicks could occasionally get lost in his sentences and become 'stuck'. Wilbur, writing in 1910, was able to interview a Doctor Jesse Green, then ninety three, who had heard Hicks speak as a child. Green told Wilbur that Hicks occasionally 'got into deep verbal water' but was always able to extricate himself.

Although Green's uncle, who was considered a good judge of public speaking, thought Hicks a very logical preacher, the Byberry Ministry is not closely argued or sharply reasoned. There is a lot of repetition in it, and this, and the rhythm of the long sentences, gives the Ministry something of the air of an incantation, or even a piece of free verse:

I have never known or witnessed any evidence of fallen angels, but those who are fallen men and women. I believe that there never were any other on this earth. Those whom the Lord has called, and who have been made partakers of the good things and power of the world to come, these when they fall away and become apostates, are fallen angels.

In his book *The liturgies of Quakerism*, Ben Pink Dandelion identifies this rhythm or cadence as a characteristic of Quaker Ministry, at least in the eighteenth century when Hicks was learning the ways of Quakerism. Such rhythms may also have found their way into the long, fluid lines of Walt Whitman's poetry.

The pattern of Hicks' words was given an extra appeal by his voice, which contemporary commentators described as 'strong', 'vibrating', and 'musical'. In a letter to Henry Wilbur, another nonagenarian, Mary Willis of Rochester, New York, described Hicks' voice as 'clear, distinct and penetrating - altogether grand'.

But what did Hicks actually say in his Byberry Ministry?

He used the analogy of a family with many children (drawing perhaps on his own experience as a father of eleven) to show how, if 'brotherly love' prevailed, there would be peace and order in the house. Hicks implies that to experience this love we must cleanse our hearts of impure thoughts and desires, 'and thus our hearts will become emptied...they will become as a vacuum' ready to be filled with divine love.

Hicks goes on to suggest that one's heart cannot be truly clear unless one is free of such things as the use of slave-goods. In this way, Hicks' Ministry moves from a discussion of the inner things of the heart and soul, to concern for the worldly actions of everyday life. At last, Hicks takes up the idea of the fallen angels, stating, as in the quotation above, that the real fallen angels are people who have wandered off the true path, and implying that the actual fallen angels of Christian mythology (and of Milton and Dante) do not exist.

There is no evidence to suggest that Hicks' Byberry Ministry was anything but acceptable to the Quakers who heard it, but certain aspects of it would not have been acceptable to any theologically conservative Anglicans, Roman Catholics or Methodists who might have read Gould's transcript. Some parts of the text are obviously heretical from an orthodox[9] Christian point of view, and others have a more subtle leaning toward heresy, as seen from an orthodox perspective.

---

[9] The word 'orthodox' (with or without a capital 'O') in this book never refers to the Eastern Orthodox Church of, for instance, Russia and Greece.

41

In talking about the impurities that stand between the Christian and his goal of a pure heart, Hicks denies the existence of the devil or of demons – beings whose existence is regularly confirmed throughout the Bible. Hicks uses the example of Mary Magdalene, from whom it is said Jesus cast out seven demons. He insists that these demons were in fact Mary's 'propensities', in other words, the sinful parts of her soul that needed to be removed. In denying the existence of fallen angels Hicks is also excluding the idea of the devil and his demons a second time, as Christian mythology suggests that these wicked creatures were once angels who became demons when they fell from heaven.

Hicks brings Adam and Eve into his discourse, but he suggests that the trees of the Garden of Eden are symbols for the wicked 'propensities' that human beings have to 'prune' and control. In suggesting that the heart or soul can be cleared of evil elements during life, Hicks is also denying the concept of original sin, and opening up the possibility that Christians can become 'established' in perfection before death. He also suggests that Scripture is not indispensable to the process of cleansing the soul, and he uses a beautiful sentence to express the inwardness of the process: 'We must come home within ourselves'. Hicks' most 'heretical' suggestion is that Jesus himself had to undergo this process of spiritual purging.

The general tendency of the Byberry Ministry,

and of much of Hicks' theology, is to boost the importance of individual Christians' own efforts to secure salvation. He also tends to downplay the role of Scripture, the teachings of the church and even of Jesus himself. It is an inward, self-reliant theology, no doubt very much suited to the lives of many of Hicks' hearers, who had to rely on their own efforts to make their way in the world as farmers, craftsmen or the owners of small businesses.

There is no doubt that if Hicks had preached such unorthodox theology in parts of medieval Europe, the authorities would have taken a shocked interest in his preaching, and poor Elias might have ended up being burned at the stake. In the Roman Catholic Europe of the middle ages, many church buildings, paintings and literary works were swarming with the 'mythological' scenes and characters, such as the Garden of Eden and the devil, that Hicks regarded as nothing more than symbols for elements in the human heart. In the United States, where religious freedom was written into the constitution, concerns about Hicks' theology became not a capital offence, but merely an internal matter for the Society of Friends.

By 1826, the misgivings of some Quakers about the Long Islander's doctrines were showing themselves in disturbances during Meetings for Worship.

In December of that year, Hicks spoke at the Meeting at Key's Alley in Philadelphia. This time the occasion began to show some of the characteristics of a stormy debate rather than a religious service.

In another piece of Ministry lasting perhaps a little under an hour, Hicks again set out his ideas about the human soul and the inward way to perfection. He identified the pure element in the human heart as the Inner Light preached by George Fox, and identified Jesus with this Light. He again played down the importance of book-learning and the work of the churches in the quest for individual redemption. He also denied the existence of heaven and hell as actual physical places, and explained why he regarded the day of judgement, as described in the New Testament Book of Revelation, as a day that will never come, as it is here inside us, exerting its influence on us every day.

The theology of this Ministry is again that of a very inward form of Christianity, and one that has been distilled, filtered and refined until many of its familiar ingredients – particularly the scriptural ones – have been left behind.

Quaker Meetings for Worship are not supposed to become debates, but the Ministry given by others after Hicks' opening speech that day in the city of William Penn was clearly designed to challenge and contradict Hicks himself.

When a man called Philadelphia Pemberton got up to speak, he hadn't even finished his first sentence before 'great confusion' broke out, and Gould, the stenographer, was unable to hear the speaker above the racket. When Pemberton's voice finally rose above the noise, Gould was able to set down his assertion that Jesus had died to save us all, that he was the only path to salvation, and that he was now sitting 'at the right hand of the Majesty in heaven, there to make intercession for us'. This heaven was, of course, the place Hicks had just denied the existence of.

Othniel Alsop was allowed to speak for about ten minutes before 'tokens of disapprobation' drowned him out. Throughout all this commotion, Hicks, who spoke three times in the course of the Meeting, tried to keep the noise down, and it would seem, from his opening choice of text, 'Peace, be still' (Mark 4:38) that he had suspected the Meeting might be a rowdy one right from the start.

The situation in the Meeting was complicated by the fact that, as Pemberton pointed out, there were many non-Quakers there, and Quakers from other Meetings, who had perhaps come just to hear Hicks, or because they suspected there might be some sort of controversy.

Painting of Hicks by Ketcham

The house at Jericho (picture by Kathryn Abbe of Jericho Monthly Meeting)

*Jericho Meeting House in the 19th Century
(Kathryn Abbe)*

Interior of Jericho Meeting House today (Kathryn Abbe)

The schoolhouse (Kathryn Abbe)

Stephen Grellet

Walt Whitman (Durham County Council)

Mount Pleasant, Ohio Meeting House
(Rea Williams)

Hicks, engraved by Peter Maverick after a painting by Henry Inman (Kathryn Abbe)

A letter to Jemima

Jericho Meeting House and school, c. 1885

Practically the same view today (Kathryn Abbe)

VI: MISGIVINGS

There had been concerns about the theology of Hicks' Ministry since 1808, when Stephen Grellet had 'laboured' with Hicks to try to get him to change his ideas. Grellet, who was Hicks' junior by twenty-five years, was from an influential French Catholic family, and had fled from the French Revolution in 1795, becoming a Quaker a year later. Grellet, like many critics of Hicks' theology, was a Quaker Minister, and a man whose views broadly coincided with the ideas behind the Evangelical Revival which had started with John Wesley's Methodism and spread to other Protestant churches.

In America, the Evangelical Revival manifested itself in the first Great Awakening, a movement for religious regeneration that was particularly associated with the preaching of the English Anglican George Whitefield, and the American Jonathan Edwards.

Although the methods of the Evangelicals were innovative, and their passion for the Gospel forever fresh, their theology was for the most part conservative. Growing up as a Catholic in France, Grellet would have been taught a theology that was not much different from that that was fervently embraced by the English-speaking Evangelicals of Britain and America.

In stark contrast to the preaching of Hicks, the Evangelicals believed in original sin – the notion that all humans are saddled with a mass of sin from birth that can never be completely washed off during life. They believed that salvation could come only through the grace of God, and that Jesus was the only path to that salvation. They also believed in the divine inspiration of the Scriptures as the word of God. The ideas of the Evangelicals were in part a religious reaction to the scepticism and rationalism of the eighteenth century.

It seems that Grellet's concerns about Hicks' preaching were at first directed only to the Long Island Quaker himself. Fourteen years later, a group of disgruntled Friends launched something like a conspiracy against him.

The plan was hatched by a section of the Philadephia Meeting for Sufferings in September, 1822. Meetings for Sufferings are so called because they were first organised to alleviate the sufferings of Quakers thrown into prison for their beliefs. Between Yearly Meetings (the annual general meetings of Quakerdom) Meetings for Sufferings are the 'standing committees' that sort out problems within a Yearly Meeting.

After a regular Meeting for Sufferings in Philadelphia, a sub-section of the Meeting met to discuss ways of stopping Elias Hicks from preaching within the bounds of Philadelphia Yearly Meeting. The upshot of this was that after Hicks had preached at the Southern Quarterly Meeting in Little Creek,

Delaware, two Friends, Ezra Comfort and Isaiah Bell, complained about Hicks' ideas to some Elders from Philadelphia who happened to be present.

Bell and Comfort had acted contrary to the correct procedure of Friends, as laid down by the Book of Discipline of Philadelphia Yearly Meeting. By rights, they should have spoken to Hicks personally about this first, then referred the matter to the Delaware Elders, not the the visiting Elders from Philadelphia.

When Hicks went on to Philadelphia, some or all of the Quakers who had met after Meeting for Sufferings 'waited on' Hicks, determined to question him about things he had preached not just in Delaware but also in New York. These were of the party that would later be called 'Orthodox' Friends. Again, Hicks' critics had acted against procedure: as Philadelphia Friends they had no right to object to Hicks' preaching in other places especially as, in accordance with Quaker custom, Hicks had up-to-date documents from his local Meetings certifying his right to travel in the Ministry.

A highly irregular meeting was proposed, to take place at the Green Street Meeting House in Philadelphia. This meeting would have been a formal confrontation between Hicks and his critics in the Philadelphia Meeting for Sufferings, but the meeting collapsed as a result of procedural disagreements. The upshot was that Hicks' critics had to be content with writing him a distinctly frosty letter, addressing him as 'thou' in the correct plain

Quaker style, and ending with the phrase, 'we cannot have religious unity with thy conduct, nor with the doctrines thou art charged with promulgating'.

In reply to this letter, Hicks simply denied that the charges in it were true, and reminded the authors of the letter that their whole proceeding was contrary to 'Gospel order'. In a further letter, endorsed by the aforementioned Jonathan Evans, Hicks' critics expanded on their accusations, and concluded with the assertion that Hicks' ideas were not consistent with those of George Fox and the early Quakers.

Throughout the controversy that was caused by some Quakers' responses to Hicks' words, the opposing parties would try to back up their points by referencing the Bible, particularly the New Testament, and the writings of early Friends. As Hicks himself knew, the New Testament contained no easy or obvious answers to such tricky theological questions as those in play among the Quakers of his time. The concerns of the first-century authors of the New Testament were not the same as those of nineteenth-century Quakers, and in any case their opinions on such matters are diverse - the New Testament is not so much a book as a small library of books written by a number of different people.

In looking to the writings of the early Quakers for their answers, the controversialists had to be very partial and selective about which texts they picked out to back up their ideas. Some early Friends, such as James Nayler, followed a very eccentric version of Christianity. Nayler himself denied the ascension of Christ, which meant that, as far as he was concerned, the body of Jesus was buried somewhere on earth and had not been taken up into heaven. George Fox's ideas were similar to those of Elias Hicks in many respects, but his famous *Epistle to the Governor of Barbados* seems to adhere to a more Evangelical viewpoint. Although some modern Quakers practically disown the Barbados letter, it is still part of the Books of Discipline of many Quaker groups.

The business of looking for theological justifications in the writings of early Friends should have been fruitless, in any case. The first Quakers deliberately avoided any set, official creed or list of doctrines - something which allowed for a wide diversity of beliefs among them. True, many statements of belief were produced by seventeenth-century Friends, but none of them acquired an official status comparable to the Roman Catholic Catechism, the Apostles' Creed or the Thirty-Nine articles of the Church of England.

An attempt was made by Orthodox Members of Philadelphia Yearly Meeting, led by Jonathan Evans, to produce something like a Quaker creed, which was inserted, very controversially, into the minutes of the Philadelphia Meeting for Sufferings. These minutes were read out at Philadelphia Yearly Meeting in the spring of 1823. This 'creed', as some came to call it, was compiled out of the writings of early (or 'primitive') Friends to justify the Evangelical point of view[10]. Many of those present at Yearly Meeting wanted this document expunged from the minutes, but a concern arose that, in simple terms, this would mess up the neat appearance of the minute-book. A compromise position was arrived at, whereby the document would remain in the minutes, but would not be put into print.

The *Extracts from the writings of primitive Friends* was, however, published as a slender pamphlet of only eleven pages, in 1823. The pamphlet was signed by Jonathan Evans as Clerk of Philadelphia Meeting for Sufferings. As its full title might suggest, it reaffirms the 'divinity of...Jesus Christ' according to the opinions of the Evangelicals, but it does this rather oddly. The printed extracts appear as separate paragraphs, unadorned with any details of where they actually came from.

The *Extracts* had first been compiled as a response to an exchange of letters that appeared in a weekly journal called the *Christian Repository*. The series started in May 1821, with an anonymous letter signed with the pen-name 'Paul'. The letter was an open one, directed 'to the Society of Friends', in which the author mentioned some aspects of Friends

---

[10] Evans, Jonathan: *Extracts from the writing of primitive Friends concerning the divinity of our lord and saviour Jesus Christ*, Solomon W. Conrad, 1823

that he admired, but then went on to express his doubts about the Quakers' tendency to cut themselves off from other denominations. In a second letter, 'Paul' expressed his reservations about the Quakers' supposed habit of paying more regard to the Inner Light than to the Bible. Soon 'Amicus', a Quaker contributor, was sending in carefully-worded replies to the letters of 'Paul'.

The version of Quakerism that 'Paul' criticised was clearly not the Evangelical version, and the version 'Amicus' defended was the version followed by Hicks. 'Amicus' was in fact a Quaker called Benjamin Ferris. Forbush tells us that there was a link between Ferris and Hicks, in that William Poole, a correspondent of Hicks', was Ferris' uncle. Poole seems to have acted as a conduit whereby Hicks' ideas could get into the 'Amicus' letters. 'Paul', it turns out, was a Presbyterian minister.

The action of the Philadelphia Meeting for Sufferings in publishing the *Extracts* was clearly an attempt to correct the impression of Quakerism that both 'Amicus' and 'Paul' were giving in their widely-read letters to the *Christian Repository*. This, and the other actions of this Meeting for Sufferings, led the Quaker historian Samuel M. Janney to claim that the greatest concentration of Evangelical critics of Hicks was to be found in that Meeting.

Janney's book on the controversies of the period[11] is clearly biased in favour of Hicks and his

---
[11] *An examination of the causes which led to the separation of*

followers, but he does respect the fact that the Evangelical Quakers were inspired by the very best intentions – it is their privileged outlook, high-handed approach and disregard for correct procedure that irritate Janney.

Janney insists that, at that crucial time, the Philadelphia Meeting for Sufferings was dominated by men who were more wealthy, worldly and urban than many of the 'country' Quakers who supported Hicks. This sociological difference is now acknowledged by modern authors, including Ben Pink Dandelion and Robert Doherty[12]. In a rather uncharitable comment, Janney insists that the Orthodox Quakers of Philadelphia included:

...a large class who had never passed through the refining process of Spiritual baptism; but being respected for their wealth, intelligence, and orderly deportment, they were appointed on committees, or employed as Clerks, until they conceived that they were qualified for service in the church, and took an active part in its discipline, without the subjection of their will to the divine government.

Despite their determination, confidence and ingenuity, the efforts of the Evangelicals up to this

the Religious Society of Friends in America 1827-28, T. Ellwood Zell, 1868

[12] Pink Dandelion, Ben: *The Quakers: A Very Short Introduction*, Oxford, 2008 and Doherty, Robert W.: *The Hicksite separation*, Rutgers University Press, 1967

point in the story seem not to have been rewarded with any real success. Their attempts to stop Hicks from preaching, and to dissociate themselves from his ideas, had been against procedure and, as a result, didn't carry enough weight to have any concrete effect. Their attempt to slip an Orthodox 'creed' into the minutes of their Yearly Meeting did not meet with the approval of that Meeting itself, and their subsequent publication of that 'creed', the *Extracts from the writings of primitive Friends*, revealed how carelessly their 'creed' had been assembled. As a document, the *Extracts* was a missed chance. Attempts by Orthodox Friends to influence the selection of Elders and other officials by local Meetings were also seen by some to be against procedure, and met with opposition. An attempt to complain directly to Hicks' local Meeting in Jericho, Long Island was also dismissed as irregular and irrelevant.

The Evangelicals or Orthodox were trying to work against the structure of Quakerdom in the United States, a structure which meant that each Yearly Meeting was a law unto itself, and could not be dominated by another Yearly Meeting, or by any higher body – in theory, there was no higher body.

This contrasts sharply with the organisation of some other Christian groups within the United States, where the various regions often have to answer to some central authority governing the entire country. In the case of the Roman Catholics, of course, the pope is the higher authority to whom the entire world-wide denomination has to defer.

The Quakers in nineteenth-century America had no such over-arching authority, although in practice the determinations of the London and Philadelphia Yearly Meetings were extremely influential, and problems such as the case of the misused New York Meeting House cellar were often referred to these Yearly Meetings which had, of course, been in existence for longer than the Yearly Meetings in, say, Ohio or Indiana.

Part of the story of Elias Hicks and his followers is the story of Members, Elders and Ministers in the newer Meetings in the U.S. resisting the influence of the senior Yearly Meetings, and particularly of the Philadelphia Meeting for Sufferings.

As the conflict deepened, the Evangelical or Orthodox Quakers started to call the followers of Hicks 'Hicksites', and the Hicksites in their turn called their opponents 'Orthodox'. Evangelical preachers such as Elisha Bates were happy to be called Orthodox, but the term 'Hicksite' is rather misleading. There is no suggestion that Elias Hicks deliberately organised a large group of non-Orthodox Quakers and elected himself as their leader. And Hicks certainly did not originate the doctrines that he preached. The name 'Hicksite' seems to have been accepted, at least by the Orthodox, because Hicks was the best-known preacher of the particular set of doctrines that the Orthodox objected to.

VII: CONFLICT

In Quaker history, most of the important events tend to happen in the various Meetings of the Society, particularly the Yearly Meetings – the AGMs of Quakerdom. These Yearly Meetings can be very large gatherings that take place over a number of days, and consist of various Business Meetings and Meetings for Worship.

The large Meetings for Business in a Quaker Yearly Meeting have to have a chairperson, and he or she has to have an assistant. In Quaker language, these important officials are called the Clerk and the Assistant Clerk. When the American Quakers started to split into Hicksite and Orthodox camps, each side tried to get people from their own party behind the Clerks' desk. Once there, the Clerks would not only chair the meeting – they would also write the minutes, which are equivalent to decisions, or recommendations for action in, say, a meeting of shareholders in a listed company.

At Philadelphia Yearly Meeting in April, 1827, an Orthodox Member called Samuel Bettle was chosen as Clerk, despite the fact that, in the Yearly Meeting as a whole, the Orthodox were in the minority. This was possible partly because the

Quakers, then and now, do not vote in their Business Meetings.

The progress of the Philadelphia Yearly Meeting that year was greatly impaired by this unpopular choice although, to its eternal glory, the divided Meeting managed to approve a huge grant of money to Friends in North Carolina, to help them evacuate freed slaves who were likely to become slaves again if they remained in that state.

While the main Yearly Meeting rumbled on at Arch Street, a fringe or alternative Meeting at Green Street, Philadelphia prepared to separate the majority Hicksite group from the minority Orthodox one in that Yearly Meeting. This was the first such separation in Quaker history. Previously, individuals or small groups had split off from the Society, sometimes because they had been disowned, but there had never before been a situation where two opposing groups both considered themselves to be Quakers, and refused to recognise the other group as anything of the sort. Seven months later, in October, 1827, the new Hicksite Yearly Meeting of Philadelphia met in a large temporary building in the city. The triumphal final minute of this meeting was signed by the Clerk – Benjamin Ferris; otherwise known as Amicus.

In the years 1827-8, the Yearly Meetings of New York, Baltimore, Ohio and Indiana also split along Hicksite/Orthodox lines. That left only three Yearly Meetings undivided. In some places, the Hicksite party were in the majority – in others, the Orthodox were. In Ohio, the numbers seem to have been about equal, which may be why the split in Ohio was particularly nasty.

Janney tells us that the Quakers of Ohio Yearly Meeting were, in effect, already divided before their 1828 Yearly Meeting began. Four of the five Quarterly Meetings had already split, and each faction of the divided 'quarters' sent their own representatives.

The Orthodox Quakers at Ohio tried to question Hicks' right to speak as a Minister at the Yearly Meeting by serving him with a paper, listing his supposed theological errors. This paper came from the Monthly Meeting of Westbury and Jericho, the tiny Orthodox faction that had formed near Hicks' Long Island home. Hicks had his own papers from the larger Hicksite bodies on Long Island, and chose to ignore the written protests of his Orthodox neighbours.

It used to be thought that Elias Hicks was not present during the chaotic scenes that were acted out in and around the Meeting House at Mount Pleasant, Ohio on the eighth of September that year. Hicks did, however, describe these events, not only in his *Journal* but also in a letter, and Paul Buckley, editor of the new edition of Hicks' *Journal*, is convinced that Hicks was there. He was certainly present at an acrimonious Meeting for Worship on the seventh of September, 1828, and there seems to be no positive evidence that he was absent on the eighth, when something like a riot occurred.

The handsome red-brick Meeting House at Mount Pleasant had been built to hold up to two thousand people, with vast shutters designed to be opened or closed to separate the men's and women's Business Meetings. On that day in 1828 the house had been decorated in advance with printed notices warning Hicks and his followers to keep out. Guards had also been appointed to exclude any Hicksites who were recognised. As the Meeting House began to fill up on that day, the press of people at the door was such that, according to Janney, many of Hicks' allies were forced to enter or be crushed or knocked over. The record of the Orthodox Minister Thomas Shillitoe asserts, however, that the Hicksites, whom he calls 'separatists', deliberately forced their way in.

As in Philadelphia, the business of the Yearly Meeting began with disagreements over the choice of Clerks, each side wanting to see its own man at the Clerks' table. The Hicksites tried to bring forward their own candidate, David Hilles, amongst much pushing and shoving. Hilles couldn't get to the Clerk's table at first, or even to the platform it stood on, but he did reach the stove in the middle of the room. There he attempted to set up camp as Clerk, and even began writing a minute. The Hicksites, however, wanted to bring him all the way to the Clerks' table, where they felt he belonged, and finally resorted to carrying him over the heads of the assembled Quakers.

The situation around the Clerks' table

degenerated as Friends clambered over the railings and came in by a door behind. Jonathan Taylor who, as Clerk of the last Yearly Meeting, was acting Clerk at the start of this one, broke one of his ribs in the crush. While all this confusion was taking place, some attempt was made to take down the names of the most disorderly participants.

As the mêlée was developing, a great cracking sound was heard from above and many people tried to rush out, believing that the gallery, or perhaps the whole building, was collapsing. The vibration of so many galloping feet caused some plaster to fall down from the ceiling, which only increased the panic.

People were knocked over and lay sprawling, in great danger of being trampled. Others dived through windows – even the upper windows. Thomas Shillitoe managed to get to a door because Friends saw that he was an old man and tried to clear a passage for him. When he got to the door he saw that it had become a bottle-neck, with a great crowd on the inside, but by this time news had spread that it was a false alarm, and things began to calm down a bit. With his carpenter's eye, Hicks noticed that the struggle over the Clerks' table had 'rendered it unfit for use'.

Shillitoe blamed the noise that had caused the stampede on a Hicksite Friend sitting in the gallery, who had snapped a piece of wood as a prank. In any case, an Orthodox Quaker called Benjamin Ladd proposed that all the members of his party should withdraw, and this is what happened. The retreat might have been a tactical mistake, as the Hicksites now remained in sole possession of the Meeting-House.

Later, the Orthodox Friends decided to hold their own separate but simultaneous Yearly Meeting, at first in the yard outside the Meeting House, and then at Short Creek Meeting House. The separation of Ohio Yearly Meeting was complete.

The Meeting House at Mount Pleasant, Ohio, built in 1814 and the first Yearly Meeting House west of the Alleghenies, still remains as a historical monument, though Quaker Meetings there were discontinued in 1909.

The separations of five Yearly Meetings in the United States had serious legal repercussions, as the various divided Quaker bodies owned a lot of property. This included Meeting Houses, schools, land and money. In his *Examination*, Janney uses the example of the Friends' Western Burial Ground in Philadelphia to show how heated the legal disputes could become.

The Western Burial Ground fell into the hands of the Orthodox faction in Philadelphia after the separation. They would not lend the key to any Hicksite Quakers, so the Hicksites had to climb in over the wall and force the locked gate from inside, in order to bury their dead. Eventually, the Hicksites resorted to making their own opening in the wall, but some of the men involved were locked up for five days for breaching the peace. Not satisfied with this limited punishment, the Orthodox went on to make an unsuccessful attempt to prosecute the Hicksite Friends involved, for trespass.

A tussle over money in New Jersey ended up in the court of chancery. The record of this trial, later published in two volumes by Jeremiah J. Foster (who held the Dickensian-sounding position of Master and Examiner in Chancery) is an important source of information on the Hicksite separation of the Quakers in America.

The Quakers of New Jersey had built up a school fund of around two thousand dollars, worth perhaps a hundred thousand dollars today. The Jersey Friends seem not to have managed to spend this money on a school or schools, but instead had lent it to a man called Shotwell, who secured the loan on some real estate. When the split happened in Philadelphia Yearly Meeting (which included New Jersey in its geographical area) the Orthodox Jersey Friends claimed the money, but Shotwell was not sure if he should pay it to them, or the new Hicksite Meeting in New Jersey. The case was referred to the Chancery Court.

It is quite against Quaker discipline and tradition to refer a dispute among Friends to a civil court, but in this case there seems not to have been any other body qualified to decide the matter. The Yearly Meetings, Meetings for Sufferings and committees that would once have handled such a case within Quakerdom were now either split or, in the case of the undivided Yearly Meetings, known to be biased toward one side.

The resulting hearings were very prolonged, as the question of which Quaker group was the authentic one could only be decided if Quaker doctrines and history were gone into in some detail.

In the end, the two judges of the case both came to the conclusion that the Orthodox Friends had a rightful claim to the money, though they arrived at this conclusion from different directions. Chief Justice Ewing said that the Orthodox must be the authentic Quaker group because the last undivided Philadelphia Yearly Meeting had had an Orthodox Clerk and a Hicksite assistant Clerk. It was this Yearly Meeting that, in Ewing's opinion, had become the Orthodox Yearly Meeting of Philadelphia.

Associate Justice Drake decided in favour of the Orthodox because, whereas they had been happy to explain their doctrines in open court, the Hicksites had refused to do so. This meant that, in Drake's mind, the Orthodox were, in effect, the winners by default.

VIII: DUST SETTLING

In Ohio, the numbers of Orthodox and Hicksites were roughly equal, but in Philadelphia, New York and Baltimore the Hicksites were in the majority. Of the divided Yearly Meetings, only Indiana had a clear Orthodox majority. New England, North Carolina and the small Yearly Meeting in Virginia remained undivided, but they continued to remain loyal to the Orthodox position of the London and Dublin Yearly Meetings, which in turn supported the Orthodox faction in the United States.

Elias Hicks' view of these melancholy events, as expressed in his *Journal*, is that the Orthodox caused the separations, having conjured up controversies about doctrine, which were only exacerbated by visiting Ministers from what Hicks calls 'old England'. Hicks puts the separations down to jealousy in the hearts of 'a few envious individuals' and says that attempts by the Orthodox to disown Friends were 'altogether out of the order of the Gospel' and therefore 'of no effect'. 'Gospel order' is an important phrase in Quakerism – roughly translated, it means 'the right way of doing things, according to our Gospel'.

In the pages of his *Journal* that deal with the

separations, Hicks only names three of his Orthodox opponents – Elisha Bates, Thomas Shillitoe and Anna Braithwaite. Of these, Shillitoe and Braithwaite were English, whereas Bates was born in Virginia, but moved to Ohio in 1817. The Virginian was forty-seven when he challenged Elias Hicks at Ohio yearly meeting in 1828, on the day before the tumultuous Meeting when the Clerks' table was broken.

On this occasion, after Hicks had spoken for a good while, Bates stood up and questioned the older man's right to be present at the Yearly Meeting at all, since Bates regarded him as, in effect, a non-Quaker. Bates went on to list some of the 'unsound' doctrines Hicks was supposed to have promoted, including his refusal to believe in the devil, or in heaven and hell, or the Garden of Eden. Bates also alleged that Hicks had denied the importance of Adam's fall, and the efficacy of Christ's Atonement for our sins on the cross.

After Bates' critique, Anna Braithwaite stood up and spoke at length on the same themes. Hicks and Bates' speeches were recorded by our old friend the stenographer M.T.C. Gould, but he was unable to hear much of what Braithwaite said, and had to find out about it later from people who *had* been able to hear.

By this time the Meeting had become restless, and many people were on their feet. Elias Hicks tried to speak again, but Bates and Braithwaite silenced him, in effect, by shaking hands and thus ending the Meeting. This misuse of the traditional end to a Meeting for Worship, when two Elders shake hands, to interrupt a speaker, was very irregular.

Hicks takes a dim view of the Ministry of Bates and Braithwaite in his *Journal*. Before the Meeting just described, Bates had challenged Hicks twice before in this way, both times in the August of 1828. On the first occasion Bates had, according to Hicks, 'made opposition to what I had communicated in a long, tedious repetition of Scripture passages'. In fact, Hicks seems to have found the preaching of Orthodox Ministers 'tedious' on many occasions.

As well as confronting him in Meetings, Bates was able to cast shade on Hicks and his followers in his role as an author, and as the owner of a magazine, published in Ohio, called the *Miscellaneous Repository*. He had also published his book *Doctrines of Friends*[13] in 1824. Bates' *Doctrines* is a text-book for Orthodox Quaker belief, and it was widely read, and reprinted in England. The popularity of the *Doctrines*, especially among Orthodox readers, is a example of Quakers, who are not supposed to have any fixed creed, taking to their hearts a text that could be used as, or regarded as, a creed.

The popularity of his *Doctrines* and his role in the separation did no harm to Bates' reputation and

---

[13] *The doctrines of Friends, or, principles of the Christian religion, as held by the Society of Friends, commonly called Quakers*, W Alexander & Son, 1829

status among the Orthodox, after the separations. When the newly-separated Orthodox Yearly Meetings held a general committee at Mount Pleasant, Ohio in 1829, Bates acted as Clerk.

The fact that Elisha Bates later drifted away from Quakerism, and was even a Methodist for a time, in no way invalidates his view of Hicks and his beliefs as stated in the 1820s. In any case, the fiery writer, publisher and printer eventually returned to Quaker Meetings for Worship and sat shyly at the back.

Anna Braithwaite, the second of the Orthodox opponents Hicks mentions in his *Journal*, had been born into the Lloyd's banking dynasty in Birmingham in 1788. The family had been Quakers from the seventeenth century: her grandfather Sampson Lloyd founded what became Lloyd's Bank in Birmingham in 1765. Her father Charles was a partner in the bank, and also a poet and anti-slavery campaigner. In 1815, at the age of twenty-seven, Anna had been recognised as a Quaker Minister.

Anna Braithwaite met Elias Hicks in 1824, on the first of her three journeys to the United States. She was then thirty-six — forty years younger than the Long Island Minister - so it is hardly surprising that during their troubled first encounter Hicks advised her that she needed more religious experience, and that such experience would help her arrive at his point of view.

Anna Braithwaite's *Memoirs* were compiled after her death from her papers, by her son Joseph Bevan Braithwaite, who was a lawyer and an important Quaker Minister in his own right. Joseph included her account of her first impressions of the Hickses, husband and wife:

His appearance is very striking — a tall thin person, with prominent eyebrows, his hair combed back...his dress like the pictures of Friends 100 years ago. His wife is also a venerable looking woman.

Despite this favourable first impression, the opinions of Hicks and Braithwaite clashed so violently that she was greatly distressed and, according to Braithwaite, Hicks was moved to tears.

Anna had come to dinner at the house in Jericho, and had a private conversation with Elias when dinner was over. Her account of this theological conversation was soon published, and something like a pamphlet war ensued, with letters, counter-letters and statements from both sides being either published or circulated in manuscript.

Anna's version accused Hicks of the same 'unsound doctrines' as those that Elisha Bates later accused him of holding at the Ohio Yearly Meeting of 1828. In a letter published in 1824[14], Hicks himself denied many of the opinions Braithwaite attributed to him, but reasserted his view that Scripture should not be the ultimate authority for a Christian, and that he did not believe that Christ's death on the cross atoned for the sins of man, which

---

[14] In *Letters & observations relating to the controversy respecting the doctrines of Elias Hicks,* 1824

Adam had brought on our heads by his fall.

Here as elsewhere, Hicks offered his own version of the central Christian narrative. Whereas Evangelicals and Orthodox Quakers believed that the Atonement was the centrepiece of the whole Christian story, Hicks believed that the key event was Pentecost. It was then that Christ's followers were given the Spirit, in the form of tongues of flame, that was to help them forge their own salvation.

Joseph Bevan Braithwaite, Anna's son and the editor of her *Memoirs*, had his own theory as to why unorthodox doctrines such as those of Elias Hicks had taken hold in America. He believed that the spread of heretical ideas was a reaction against the unyielding orthodoxy of the Pilgrim Fathers.

At least Anna Braithwaite dared to enter Hicks' house, despite her feelings of trepidation:

I thought on first entering the house, my heart and flesh would fail, but after a time of inexpressible conflict, I felt a consoling belief that best help would be near...

Two years later, the English Quaker minister Thomas Shillitoe refused an invitation proffered by Hicks himself, standing out in front of his own house as he often did to welcome strangers. Shillitoe had been under the impression that the Hicksites meant to claim him as one of their own, and in his own *Journal* he tells us that, on his passage across the Atlantic, he twice had a vision of a man who was to meet him when he landed in New York, whose brain was full of 'combustible matter' to pour out on Shillitoe. After he had these visions, he felt some assurance that God would protect him from this man, whom Shillitoe presumably took to be Elias Hicks. At a Meeting for Worship at Hicks' home Meeting House at Jericho, the English Minister felt that Hicks' words were intended as a snare – one he was able to avoid.

Shillitoe was a Londoner, brought up as an Anglican, who took to Quakerism in his teens. He left his job in a Quaker bank in Lombard Street because the bank handled lottery tickets, which was a contradiction of the Quaker testimony against games of chance. Thomas then took up the profession of shoemaker, and was so successful that he was able to establish an annuity that would give him £100 a year. Planning to live on this modest income, he retired from business in 1806, at the age of fifty-two.

Shillitoe travelled as a Quaker Minister all over Britain and Ireland, and around continental Europe and America. He preached in taverns, prisons and palaces; in Europe he spoke with, among others, both the King and the Crown Prince of Prussia, the King of Denmark and the Tsar of Russia. He was a pioneering teetotaller and vegetarian – a wiry, energetic figure.

Where he appears in Hicks' *Journal*, Thomas Shillitoe cuts a rather pathetic figure. The first encounter we hear about was at the Monthly Meeting in July, 1828 at Westland (near Brownsville, Pennsylvania). Here Shillitoe stood up to oppose Hicks after he had spoken: Hicks subsequently wrote that on this occasion he was 'truly sorry for the old Friend for (if he goes on in the way he is now in) he will not only expose himself to the ridicule of the people, but will become a reproach to the Society' (it was a little unfair of Hicks to call the English Quaker an 'old Friend', as Shillitoe was actually his junior by six years).

In his own *Journal*, Shillitoe asserts that at Westland he had risen to speak in order to assure the non-Quakers who were present that many 'sound' Quakers, as Shillitoe called them, did not, like Hicks, disbelieve the New Testament story of the miraculous conception of Christ. Shillitoe also questioned Hicks' assertion that Quakers should not set one day a week aside as a sabbath. After Shillitoe had finished, Hicks stood up and argued against the sabbath idea. Shillitoe then rose and spoke again, and seems to have believed that he had silenced Hicks with his arguments. This type of debate characterised Hicks' later encounters with Shillitoe, in both Pennsylvania and Ohio. Like Bates and Braithwaite, Shillitoe was also present at the tumultuous Ohio Yearly Meeting of 1828.

Perhaps the most important of Hicks' Orthodox critics was the aforementioned Stephen Grellet, who is not, however, mentioned by Hicks in his *Journal*.

Like Thomas Shillitoe, Grellet had also toured continental Europe, and had meetings with the Russian Tsar and the King of Prussia. Grellet also met the pope and the king of Spain. It was the same Grellet who first alerted the Quaker prison reformer Elizabeth Fry to conditions in Newgate prison – a warning that eventually led Fry into the great work of her life.

For Orthodox Quakers like Grellet, the mass of Hicksite Friends who separated from his own party were in effect lost to the Society of Friends, and in places like Hicks' old stomping-ground of Long Island, Grellet could see very few people he could count as Quakers at all. Returning to the Island after the separation, he wrote:

I then crossed over to Long Island, where I had meetings with the small remnants of our society. Very little companies are left in those parts, where lately there were many Friends.

Of New York City Orthodox Friends he wrote:

Friends were deeply baptised together into suffering; for in all their particular meetings, they have shared the same bitter cup...This sore trial in our Society, which, through a spirit of unbelief, has plunged many into gross darkness, has tended to bring others to an increase of faith in...God, and of our Lord Jesus Christ.

It was probably in 1828, when much of American

Quakerdom was breaking apart like an unfired pot, that the poet and fellow Long-Islander Walt Whitman saw Elias Hicks preach in the unlikely setting of the ballroom of a Brooklyn Heights hotel. Whitman was about nine at the time, but his memory of Hicks remained with him for at least sixty years. The ballroom, which was as fancy as a glitter-ball and full of dignitaries from the area, must have contrasted sharply with what Whitman calls the 'grim' Friends on the platform.

Whitman was impressed by Hicks' 'tall, straight figure', 'forehead of great expanse and large and clear black eyes'. In his *November boughs* he recounts how the Long Island preacher used his 'resonant, grave, melodious voice' and 'magnetic stream of natural eloquence' to convince 'all minds and natures, all emotions, high or low, gentle or simple'. As his oratory warmed up, Hicks 'takes the broad-brim hat from his head, and almost dashing it down with violence on the seat behind, continues with uninterrupted earnestness'.

Several times during his Ministry at Morrison's Hotel in Brooklyn, Hicks fell 'into the nasality and sing-song tone sometimes heard in such meetings' but then stopped and resumed 'in a natural tone'.

Whitman identified Hicks as one of the world's rare spirits – water from a 'perennial spring' sent to 'irrigate the soil':

Always Hicks gives the service of pointing to the fountain of all naked theology, all religion, all worship, all the truth to which you are possibly eligible – namely yourself and your inherent relations...he is the most democratic of the religionists - the prophets...

It would seem from this assessment that Whitman saw something of himself in Elias Hicks, or that he projected some of his own personality onto his image of the old man. The poet understood that the Quaker emphasised the inner, heart-felt aspect of Christianity, and this could be said to resemble Whitman's own view of the self as a sort of brimming jug of potentialities. It was, after all, Whitman who wrote the poem *Song of myself,* and included in it the line; 'Walt Whitman, a cosmos, of Manhattan the son'.

In his *November boughs* Whitman even comes close to comparing Hicks to Jesus, though in a tortuous and unclear sentence:

We can briefly say, summarily, that his whole life was a long religious missionary life of method, practicality, sincerity, earnestness, and pure piety - as near to his time here, as one in Judea, far back - or in any life, any age.

Whitman's interest in Quakerism was part of his birthright: his mother Louisa was from a Quaker background, and the poet was very close to his Quaker grandmother, Amy Williams Van Velsor, whose death when Walt was only ten was a source of great sadness to him. As well as Quakerism in his past, Whitman would also have had a lot of Quakerism in his present, not least because of the number and influence of Quakers on his home turf of Long Island and New York.

Whitman often uses Quaker language in his poetry, including the old Quaker names for the months (for example 'first month' for January). His anti-war and anti-slavery sentiments may also have grown out of his Quaker background: the treatment of the American Civil war in both his poetry and his prose often has a realism and compassion which resembles the very best of the Quaker spirit.

In his prose, Whitman often touches on Quaker themes, and in *November boughs* he even attempts an account of the origins of Quakerism.

Whitman was not only drawn to Quaker preachers on his regular 'jaunts' either side of the East River. He was something of a collector of celebrities, or, as he calls them, 'celebres'. New York and Brooklyn were the kinds of places one would have expected to see such people in those days, and Whitman managed to get a good long look at Abraham Lincoln, James Fenimore Cooper, the millionaire John Jacob Astor, and Lafayette, among others. He also had a conversation with Edgar Allan Poe, finding him 'subdued, perhaps a little jaded'[15].

---

[15] From Whitman's *Autobiographia*

IX: LAST DAYS

Elias Hicks was eighty years old at the time of the acrimonious separation in Ohio, and not in the best of health. For a long time he had suffered from 'gravel', meaning kidney-stones, which, intermittently, caused him a lot of pain. In 1824 he had what he calls in his *Journal* 'a severe attack of bodily indisposition', which Buckley takes to mean a heart-attack.

In 1829 Hicks brought home a fever which his wife Jemima caught – within a few days, she was dead. By this time, Hicks had lost all four of his sons, two of his daughters and at least two of his grandchildren.

His friend William Poole had suggested that Hicks compile a journal as early as 1823, but Hicks resisted it, suspecting that such a book might be of little use to later generations. At first sight, this might look like false modesty, but it was in fact a manifestation of one of Hicks' beliefs – that each generation would experience the Spirit in a different way. This was one reason for his suspicion of the Scriptures and of traditional doctrines – with his large, intelligent ears he was listening out for something new.

Despite his reservations Elias did, however, put together what became his *Journal,* in the last year of his life. This he did by sitting at home at his fine cherry-wood desk and drawing on travel diaries, and a home journal covering the years from 1813-1819.

Readers expecting an autobiography of the Long Island minister that concentrates on the more controversial episodes of his life will be disappointed by the *Journal* of Elias Hicks. What Hicks offers us is an account of his life that emphasises his Ministry, much of which happened before he became a controversial figure. Even where it covers the years of the greatest controversy among the Friends in the 1820s, the *Journal* says amazingly little about the huge events that surround the author. What is left is an account of extensive travels in the Ministry, in the course of which Hicks was usually able to make his hearers accept the message God had given him to deliver.

In his *November boughs*, Walt Whitman advises interested readers to buy Hicks' *Journal* 'at some Quaker book-store', despite what he calls its 'dryness and mere dates, absence of emotionality or literary quality'.

A large pattern is repeated in those parts of the *Journal* that relate the details of Hicks' travelling Ministry. At first, Hicks feels drawn to travel in the Ministry to some place – usually quite a large area with a number of settlements. He obtains certificates of approval of his plan from his local Meetings, and sets off, usually with a companion.

Having arrived, he attends Business Meetings and Meetings for Worship in the area in question – also so-called 'appointed' Meetings are usually arranged for him. These 'appointed' Meetings are outside of the usual Quaker routine of Meetings, and are set up merely so that Hicks can give Ministry.

Throughout Hicks' *Journal*, we hear of Meetings happening in large buildings, some of them not Quaker Meeting Houses at all, where the place is nevertheless overcrowded. Towards the end of the *Journal*, Hicks and his followers are sometimes kept out of Quaker buildings by Orthodox Friends, and are forced to meet in the open air.

The majority of Meetings Hicks describes are successful in that he is given a message to put across, and his hearers find his message acceptable. Often those present at the Meeting are humbled by the experience, but the ultimate effect is one of satisfaction and comfort.

Like many Quaker Ministers who wrote journals, Hicks does not really write about what his own wisdom, will or talent enabled him to do – as far as he is concerned, all his long-lived success as a Minister was an undeserved gift from God.

Buckley believes that before it could be published, the *Journal* was edited by Members of the Meeting for Sufferings of the Hicksite Yearly Meeting of New York. In his painstaking edition of the *Journal*, Buckley tracks the alterations through footnotes. In the sections dealing with the separations, the original editors seem to have tried to pull the teeth of the text by excluding the names of specific opponents of Hicks, and removing whole paragraphs which describe his confrontations with his critics. It is to be hoped that Buckley's unexpurgated version will give a new generation of readers a clearer idea of the life and labours of Hicks as related in his own words.

On February 14th, 1830, Elias Hicks suffered a stroke after writing his last letter – a rousing message of religious hope directed to his friend Hugh Judge. As he lay in bed partially paralysed, he used what little movement he still had to push off a cover that had been placed over him. At first his carers did not understand this, but then they realised that the coverlet was made of cotton. Hicks died on February 27th and was laid to rest next to Jemima in the burial ground of the Jericho meeting house. We know that, at first, he was not allowed to rest in peace.

Select Bibliography

A series of extemporaneous discourses, delivered in the several meetings of the Society of Friends...by Elias Hicks, J. & E. Parker, 1825

Bates, Barnabas: *Remarks on the character and exertions of Elias Hicks on the abolition of slavery: being an address delivered before the African Benevolent societies in Zion's Chapel, New-York, March 15, 1830.* New York, 1830

Bates, Elisha: *The doctrines of Friends, or, principles of the Christian religion, as held by the Society of Friends, commonly called Quakers*, W Alexander & Son, 1829

Bownas, Samuel: *A Description of the Qualification Necessary to a Gospel Minister,* Pendle Hill Publications, 1989

Braithwaite, Anna; Hicks, Elias, et al: *Letters & observations relating to the controversy respecting the doctrines of Elias Hicks,* 1824

Braithwaite, Anna: *Memoirs of Anna Braithwaite*, Headley Brothers, 1905

Canby, Henry Seidel: *Walt Whitman: An American,* Houghton Mifflin, 1943

Doherty, Robert W.: *The Hicksite separation,* Rutgers University Press, 1967

Drake, Thomas E: *Quakers and Slavery in America,* Yale University Press, 1950

Forbush, Bliss: *Elias Hicks: Quaker Liberal,* Columbia University Press, 1956

Fox, George: *The Journal of George Fox,* Everyman, 1924

Freiday, Dean: *Barcley's Apology in Modern English,* The Barclay Press, 1991

Evans, Jonathan: *Extracts from the writing of primitive Friends concerning the divinity of our lord and saviour Jesus Christ,* Solomon W. Conrad, 1823

Hicks, Elias: *The Journal of Elias Hicks,* Inner Light Books, 2009

A history of Prince Lee Boo, to which is added, the life of Paul Cuffee, a man of colour, also, some account of John Sackhouse, the Esquimaux, C. Crookes, 1820

Janney, Samuel M.: *An examination of the causes which led to the separation of the Religious Society of Friends in America, 1827-28*, T. Ellwood Zell, 1868

Jones, Rufus M.: *The Later Periods of Quakerism*, Volume I, Macmillan, 1921

Jones, Rufus M.: *The Quakers in the American Colonies*, Norton, 1966

LeMaster, J.R. and Cummings, Donald D., eds. *Walt Whitman, an encyclopedia*, Garland, 1998

Noll, Mark A.: *The rise of Evangelicalism*, Apollos, 2004

'Paul' and 'Amicus': *Letters of Paul and Amicus, originally published in the Christian Repository*, Robert Porter and Joseph Rakestraw, 1823

Pink Dandelion, Ben: *The Liturgies of Quakerism*, Ashgate, 2005

Pink Dandelion, Ben: *The Quakers: A Very Short*

Introduction, Oxford, 2008

Punshon, John: *Portrait in Grey: A Short History of the Quakers*, QHS, 1984

Shillitoe, Thomas: *Journal of the life, labours and travels of Thomas Shillitoe in the service of the Gospel of Jesus Christ*, Vol. II, Harvey and Darton, 1839

Traubel, Horace, *With Walt Whitman in Camden*, Gay & Bird, 1906

Webb, Simon: *George Fox in Barbados: With the Complete Text of the Letter to the Governor of Barbados*, Simon Webb, 2006

Whitman, Walt: *Autobiographia: selected from his prose writings*, Putnam, 1892

Whitman, Walt: *November Boughs*, Kessinger, 2004

Wilbur, Henry Watson: *The Life and Labours of Elias Hicks*, Friends General Conference Advancement Committee, 1910

Woolman, John: *The Journal and Other Writings of John Woolman*, Dent, 1952

Made in the USA
Columbia, SC
06 July 2025